THE ARTS OF BEING A STRONG WOMAN

Twenty Habits of Every Strong Woman

Emily Chase

©Emily Chase

Contents

INTRODUCTION

Beloved, let's say goodbye to an era where you live your life on the dictates of others. Where you can't tell which conduct you are to adopt. Where you don't know either to be yourself or be what others want you to be. You are a woman and you are a Strong woman, therefore let's explore what Strong women do together so you could see how to reshape your life and live to fulfill your dreams.

The target is that you live the life of your choice, and that you are happy. And most importantly, you fulfill your dreams.

CHAPTER ONE

SELF APPRECIATION

Strong women have certain things they do differently, but it all begins with understanding and appreciating themselves. You must know yourself because there is no way you can successfully build your unique self if you do not understand yourself, your body, your qualities and all about you. After this you appreciate your qualities because being strong is not only realizing who you are, it is about accepting and loving who you are. Really, if you do not know yourself who will? If you do not appreciate yourself, if you

have no self-worth, no self-love, if you

do not value yourself who will? It all

begins with you and you.

Now let's have a look on the habits of

strong women who are on the journey of

knowing and appreciating themselves,

what do they do differently?

HABIT 01

UNDERSTAND YOUR NATURE.

Beloved do you know that even if you are a twin you are not going to be exactly the same as your twin? Even when you are identical twins you have differences in the way you receive, absorb and process details. You have different ideas and your body reacts differently to things. And this is why you need to know who you are, understand your nature, understand yourself, understand your mind and emotions and how all this can affects your actions.

We as humans don't have equal body and

mental strength, we get stressed out in different ways, our body reacts to things differently and our brain processed Information differently. When you understand this, then you are on the journey of mastering the arts of Strong women. When you understand your nature and accept it as it is you wouldn't hate yourself, you wouldn't wish to be like others. You will simply do things that fit your nature, you will grow and thrive.

APPRECIATE YOUR UNIQUE QUALITIES

Every individual is unique and we have what distinguishes us from others. Strong women hammer on their unique qualities, they understand that they can't be perfect in every aspects. Therefore they look for those little things they are good at and put their strength in them and turn them to mighty things.

Your unique qualities need not be great things, but you can turn them to great things. Appreciate yourself for those things you can do, it might be that you are good cook or you have a gentle nature, it can be a great sense of humor, it can be the ability to give good advice. The lists doesn't end, understand these qualities in you and appreciate yourself for having them. Strong women appreciate themselves, having understood that there is only a version of you, that you are unique then it is a must for you to appreciate the little things you can do. Again this need not be great things or achievement, it will be very wrong for you to wait till you are great or when you do great things before you appreciate yourselves. Appreciate the little things, little things is what grow to be bigger things.

HABIT03

SELF LOVE.

A strong woman knows the importance of herself, she values and loves herself. Self-love is the regards for one well-being and happiness. Often people advise you to put others first, to be selfless.

Well, strong women are not selfish but they understand the need to put themselves first, to love and care for themselves because they understand that this is the beginning to a happy and healthy life. If they do not care for themselves, who will? So while you are on the process of being strong. You must learn to love yourself. Accept yourself for who you are and be proud of yourself, this includes celebrating the little wins and accepting your flaws.

In order to achieve self-love you need to talk to yourself about love, and when talking to others about yourself talk with love. Let it be obvious that you care for yourself and have regard for yourself. This include having trust in yourself and your abilities, being true and nice to yourself, do not move or work with people that consider you inferior and would ensure to do things that will make you feel inferior set boundaries while still being kind. Do kind and nice things, things that you will be proud of, that you will tap yourself and say "I am a good woman"

Do not minimize the good things about yourself, forgive yourself and overlook your shortcomings; do not let your past failures define who you are. Appreciate your worth and values, in simple terms, give yourself the love you deserved.

HABIT 04

SELF ESTEEM

Self-esteem is the confidence in one's worth and abilities.   This is a very important art that must be mastered by every woman. When you lack self-esteem then you should know that many things won't fall into it place.

Without self-esteem you can't attain your goal, your psychological health will also be at risk because lack of self-esteem leads to self-rejection which often causes depression.

To live a healthy life, one must have a high self-esteem and regard for oneself. Do not see yourself as inferior to others. Accept your flaws; understand that no one is perfect and that mistakes are bound to happen.

Strong women have great regards for themselves, they see themselves as great and important. They know they are valuable and they respect themselves. They don't let the opinions of others break them, they put themselves first and nourish themselves with the things that really matters to them. They call themselves good names and describe themselves with positive words.

Therefore honey, part of your strengths lies in how you view yourself, what you think of yourself and how you regard yourself. You will never achieve your aim of being strong if you do not place yourself high. Therefore honey, love who you are and be strong. And

this is a duty you owe yourself.

HABIT05

ACCEPT YOUR WEAKNESS

No one is perfect, of course you must have heard this a thousand and one times, well it will be a great mistake to think Strong women are set of Perfect women. No, but rather they are women who accept that they have weakness but wouldn't let that define them rather they try to work on their weakness and strive to become better persons.

Accepting your weakness is part of self-appreciation, you are not deceiving yourself and you are not feigning to be what you are not. Rather you are open to yourself, you let yourself knows there are things you might not be able to do or perhaps things that isn't easy for you to do. When you do this you are able to work better on this weakness and turn it into strength. I had a friend in university that didn't assimilate and understand what she studied quickly compared to the rest of us, however she accepted this, she didn't hate herself for it neither did she consider herself a blockhead. Rather she set a timetable for studying, she used to read more than the rest of us, she knew she can't read it all a week or two weeks to examination and understand it so she read for few hours every day. This helped her so much that before we knew it she was almost better than the remaining of us as regards academics, she was never afraid of lecturers asking random questions in class or setting us impromptu test. Well at the end she was one of the best students in my class. Do you know why? No honey, it wasn't because she read every day, it was because she understood her nature and accepted it. She was in other words, a strong woman.

CHAPTER TWO

RELATIONSHIP WITH OTHERS

The ways we relate with others have a lot to do with us and the type of person we are building ourselves to be. This is because there are different kinds of people with different manners, some are kind and will always respect others and treat them with the honor they deserve whereas some are selfish and filled with hatred for others, especially to those who fail to subscribe to their beliefs or who does not allow them to dictate what to do and what not for them.

Strong women understand the different kind of people that we have, they know there are many who will try to look down on them and try to force them do things against their will. They know there are those who will try to make them feel inferior and try to make them disregard themselves, those who will laugh at their dreams and try to play with their weakness. But strong women do not allow these people to break them. They know what they want and that is their focus. They have their habits with different people; they simply take their time to learn the best way to deal with different kind of people.

HABIT06

SHE IS KIND AND GENEROUS

A Strong woman does not look down at others. She is kind and generous, she treats people in a good way and helps them in the way she can.

Strong woman is nice and hospitable. She is not hostile or arrogant, she is accommodating. Being kind is one of the characteristics of a strong woman; she isn't hostile or proud to others, even when she has attained the peak of her achievements she is friendly to others and always ready to help. She simply wants to fill the world with her light and empathy. Her relatives, husband, children, friends, neighbors and acquaintances all know her to be a good woman.

When she is capable of doing things to alleviate other people's distress she will never hesitated in doing so. She knows the importance of being good and she does not care with the fact that there will be those whom out of hatred will not appreciate her. She know it is their loss not hers, she is lighthearted and filled with happiness while those who hate her and are jealous of her will be filled of hatred, sadness and light of progress. She knows she has nothing to lose for being kind. It only makes her a better person.

Therefore beloved, your journey to being a strong woman won't be complete until you incorporate the act of kindness and generosity into it. You are a queen; you are simply a strong woman.

SHE DOESN'T LIVE HER LIFE ON THE DICTATES OF OTHERS.

A lot of people live their life on the dictates of others directly or indirectly, they told you to go to school or learn a particular skill or get married or have certain Number of kids. What to do and what not to do. Or they set a standard for her; expect her to go through a particular line of conducts. Have a particular shape, face made up, wear particular types of clothing etc.

Different communities have different standards set out for women, some communities want their woman to only care about her facial look, to these people all that matters is her facial and physical appearance, her job is to look attractive to men when they see her, she should be able to control men with her looks.

Whereas strong women know and understand that beauty is far beyond facial beauty. While they take their time to care for their look, they equally build themselves as a whole, their character, their future, their happiness and their dreams. They do not allow others to impose how to live on them. They are wise and always try to make the best decisions for themselves.

There are people whom out of hatred and

jealousy of others try to ridicule them by mocking them and playing with their weakness. It can be financial weakness or any types of weakness and shortcomings; they try to force them to do things against their interest but Strong women live based on her dreams and happiness, based on what she is capable of, what she will excel at.

A woman might want to reach the peak of Schooling; another might want to excel in a certain art. Both are Strong women as long as they are pursuing their dream and happiness

HABIT08

SHE KNOWS WHEN TO SAY NO.

There should always be a boundary, Strong women know when and how to set boundaries. She knows when to say no to others. Although she is nice and approachable she does not allow others take her for granted.

When she can't do a particular task or when it will be inconvenient for her. She says No rather than putting herself in uncomfortable situations. While she listened to good advice from people, she does not allow herself and her weakness to be toyed with. Because she is a woman that has understood herself and accepts herself for who she is, she does not allow others plan her life for her. When she is able to do something she does it, but when she can't she simply says no.

She does not overburden herself, she takes good care of her mental health, she knows that if she put other first and do things beyond her capacity to satisfy them, in the end if she fails she would be left alone, the people whom she ruined her life to satisfy would not be there for her, in fact these will be the first people to mock and laugh at her. A Strong woman takes care of her mental health.

HABIT09

CONFIDENCE

By taking calculated actions, Strong women build Confidence in their self. They are able to stand tall and make eye Contact with their correspondence.

Others could see the Confidence in them. Strong women believes in themselves, you see this when you look at them, they are sure of themselves and their abilities. This is what you see when you look at a Strong woman but behind this are many failures, many fidgeting, many practices. So to develop Confidence in yourself, know that you have to plan, make conscious and calculated decisions.

One thing I have found out is that when are confident and people can see the confidence in you they respect you and check the kind of words they say to you. They know you are not scared of them so they can't control you; humans are like that, when they know someone is weak and is afraid of them they do more to increase the fear by suppressing the person. They maltreat him and take him for granted, being certain that he can't fight back. But they can't play the same game with a confident person, because they know they can't control him. Therefore beloved, part of your strength lies in being confident.

Do not be scared of people; face them with your heads up. Talk to them although with respect but without fear, do not shiver or fidget while talking to other humans. This is something you achieved overtime with practice and it is also achievable when you take calculated steps to improve yourself and work on your achievement. No doubt humans respect those with good standings in the   society.

BUILDING OTHERS UP

A Strong woman is not selfish they care for others and know that the Success of others will not affect their own. They are there for other women and even men, for both the old and young. They just want to see the world become a better place.

Strong women know that they lose nothing by building others up and that if anything they only improve themselves by it. They understand the struggles of achieving ones goal and are ready to guide and help others in achieving theirs. They are not harsh neither are they proud nor arrogance. People lower than them in worldly achievements can easily go to them for advise and mentorship. They are usually there to help either with words and in other ways they can. They hate people being trampled upon or being denied of their rights, they understand that all humans have fundamental rights which should be respected. They do not keep quiet when others are being abused; they raised their voice and act.

CHAPTER THREE

PURSUING YOUR GOALS

There are many reasons you should never give up on your goals, no matter the difficulties you are passing through or how hard or difficult to achieve it seems. This is because one of the things that make you happy is pursuing your dreams, and people often judge others based on their stands and achievement. However your goals should be things that actually make you happy and not just what others are doing. You should choose careers that fits your nature and resonates with you, something that will not only bring you income but improve your general happiness, that wouldn't wear you out or disturb your mental health. There are many of these, all you have to do beloved is to sit, plan and come out with as many as you are able to find. And when you do find them, set for yourself the path of achieving them   and   these.

HABIT11

COURAGE

Show me a Courageous woman and I will show you a strong woman. A strong woman has courage to go for what she wants. Firstly, she knows what she wants and she is not scared of pursuing it. She knows there will be obstacles and she knows she might not have Supporting hands around her. But she does give up regardless of these; she is ready to pass through the difficulties to achieve her aim.

I don't want to use the "nothing good comes easy" phrase but I will be saying that achieving your purpose in life requires hard work and dedication. You need to be courageous and face the task and challenges. You shouldn't give up because of the challenges you will face, there will be obstacles no doubt, but part of your strength as a strong woman lies in being progressive and being consistence with the things you are doing. Again it need not be many things at a time, what matter is that you are progressing, and a little progress is far better to being stagnant.

HABIT 12

SHE PURSUE HER DREAM AND INTEREST

One of the defining factors of being a Strong woman is the ability to pursue your dreams and Interest. They can be hard to achieve but you keep on pursuing it. You try your best, you know the things that matters to you and those to cancel in order to achieve your aim. The main thing is not giving up on your dreams, no doubt there would be times when you will feel like letting go and living like others, but beloved you must be aware that you are not others, your goal and ambitions are part of the things that make who you are, so be strong and never give up. People will come with different plans for you, but you alone know where your interest and capacities lies, and this you should always pursue.

There might be situations where you won't be able to completely go against the plans of others especially if you are still dependent on them financially but even in these instances, you should not let go of your dreams because at the end of it all what matters is your mental health and happiness. I have a friend whose father was bent on his studying medicine and become a medical doctor but he was someone that doesn't have great regards for this, he simply did not have the strength for it. He wanted a cool life, he wanted to do something he is good at and what he has interest in.   but he knew the whole family would go against him and he wasn't ready for that, he didn't even have any source of finance for him to pursue what he want. So what did he do?

He opt in for medicine and was doing what he could with it, then he started pursuing his interest too, he wanted to be a programmer, his father got him a system upon admission to university and it was helpful for him, for five years he was building and pursuing his interests. Before he left medical school he had achieved his goal, he was making money already and could stand on his own.

Well at the end of the day, no one care whether he practiced medicine or doing some other works, what mattered to everyone and even his father was that he is successful, rich and well known in his community.

So beloved, never give up on your interests and ambitions, be strong and be wise.

HABIT 13

PURSUE YOUR HAPPINESS

Strong women know what they are about. They do things that make them happy. They understand that other people might not understand or care for their need to happiness but Strong women do not care about other's opinion. They know the things that make them happy and they pursue it Their happiness also do not depend on the downfall of others, they are not in Competition with anyone. Their aim is to improve themselves and become a better person. And their happiness depends in achieving their aims.

Being happy is very essential and in fact one of the most important things in life. You can have all the money in this life and not be a happy person. That is why you should go for the things you like and that make you happy. I always tell people that if a job that offers "five hundred dollar" per months makes you more happy and have enough time to do the other things that matter to you, and also gives you time to care for your mental health then chose it over another job that offers one thousand dollar but which you only take for the sake of the money. Money isn't everything, strong women know this, they know the importance of being happy and they never compromise this for any reason.

HABIT 14

BOLDNESS

Being bold is one of the characteristics of a strong woman, boldness does not necessarily denote being extroverted, social or outgoing. A bold woman can be an introverted woman who has trust in herself and her abilities. She takes risks and act innovatively. She accepts herself for who she is and not let society dictates for her. There are households where women are expected to be outspoken, or follow a particular rule of conduct. A strong woman understands her nature and she goes for what fits her. She is also bold in pursuing her goals and interests, she faced whatever obstacles comes her way fiercely, and she does not let it break her or make her give up. She is bold and always take bold steps, she knows that part of her strength lies in not been scared or afraid of obstacles.

HABIT 15

SHE KNOWS HER FEMININE POWER AND HOW TO USE IT.

Women are Strong creatures look at how we carry another human being for nine months, give birth and take care of him the many sleepless night of caring and nurturing another human.

Women are naturally gifted and they can control men without necessarily commanding. The nature of women is unique, Strong women understand this and know when to use her power to achieve her desire without hurting others or ruining her modesty and chastity. She use her feminine power to do great things and achieve her goals.

Again using your feminine power does not mean using your body to lure men or the like rather feminine power lies in creativity, gracefulness, and art of listening, protecting and nurturing. All these can be used and put together to achieve your goal and increase your general power. Think about your kindness, emotion, love, gentleness and intuition and how embracing and making use of them would increase your general happiness and help in reaching your target.

CHAPTER FOUR

HANDLING DIFFICULT SITUATIONS

A poet writes that life is made of joy and woes, and how true these words are, there are times in life where we will be happy, glad and excited due to the happy things occurring in our lives and there are times we will be sad, perplexed and depressed, also due to the sad things happening in our lives. These are two situations that are bound to happen to everyone, regardless of who you are and what you are. And strong women are not left out but as a strong woman, how do you handle hard times and difficulties? What

kind of response do you give to it?

SHE UNDERSTANDS WHAT PERFECTION IS.

Strong women know that Perfection is a gradual and continuous process. She keeps on improving herself until she is faultless, this might take many years and it is a lifelong effort. She knows that real Perfection is in not giving up.

She knows she has to work towards Perfection and she has to keep striving for it. She understand that things might be hard and life might at some point toss what will make her wearied and tired, she knows this does not mean she is less of a strong woman but rather that it is life's doings and it can befall anyone. Perfection does not lie in not being afflicted but rather in the way one handles affliction. She is patient and she perseveres, she does not blame herself over what she has no control over, she accepts the situation and look for ways to overcome it.

HABIT17

SHE KNOWS WHEN TO LET GO.

Strong women do not hold onto things that doesn't add values to them, it does not matter whether this is a friendship, relationship or acquaintanceship. Or whether it is even plans and goals they set for themselves in the past.

She knows when to let go and move on, she believes what is meant for her won't miss her and that which missed her wasn't meant for her.

She does not hold grudges or hate people about, instead she free herself from them and move on with her life. She understands that certain things and people might not be meant for her, she does not hate herself for not been able to keep to them, she simply let go when she no longer matters to them. This is easier to do when she already has a purpose and has many things to keep and make her happy. Her happiness does not depend on other people, she is a happy woman who engaged herself in many things that makes her happy.

She knows how to go, she does not hold on or has fake hope in things that are not meant for her, she also understand that letting go after being betrayed by others is not an easy task, therefore she allowed herself the time to cry ,the time to mourn, the time to heal

and   the   time   to   move   on.

HABIT18

SHE HOLD FIRM TO HER FAITH

Strong women recognize the greatness of God in their life and she hold firm to her faith and her belief. When she is down she prays to her lord and He is her helper, her Consoler. Strong women do not let others force them out of their belief. They live by it and attain their strength through it.

When difficult times come they go on their knee and pray to their creator, they know and understand that even if the entire world should forsake them the one that created them wont. They are certain of His love for them and they call unto him in difficult times. During the times of ease and happiness they give thanks to Him. They know they can always reach out to Him anytime and any day without any intermediary.

HABIT 19

SHE KNOWS HOW TO HANDLE HARD TIMES

Hard times come and go, Strong women know this and they understand that there is no joy without woe. Life is made of joy and woes; there will always be a mixture of these two.

A Strong woman prepares for hard times, and when hard times hit her unprepared, she faced it with braveness. She does not blame herself unnecessarily. She learnt from her mistakes and work on being a better person.

Life cannot be all rosy no matter how great you are trying and Preparing, financial distress might occur, or loss of a beloved one or betrayal of trust, the list does not end. As a Strong woman you need to accept this, but rather than swimming in the pool of self-blame or regrets, you find your way out of the mess and move on.

Again everyone knows facing and dealing with hard times aren't easy, one of the best thing you can do is occupying yourself with other things that can improve who you are as a person, rest, relaxed your mind and know that it is a phase that will come and go.

HABIT20

SHE KNOWS THERE IS ONLY ONE VERSION OF HERSELF. SHE IS A QUEEN IN HER OWN LANE.

Strong women know there is only a version of themselves, not only do they have different facial looks, their mind and body differs too. A Strong woman works on herself, she values herself, she classes herself and love herself. She has her goals laid out, she gently climb the ladder, gently but steadily.

She is a Queen, she wouldn't let anyone tell her Otherwise, therefore her honor, dignity and respect matters to her and this she command and earn from others.

CONCLUSION

Women can be Strong in different ways and with different habits. This is because no two women are the same and we all have different natures and dispositions. Also, we go through different trials and difficulties which have impacts on the type of responses we will give it.

However, this book try to cover the general habits of Strong women and how we as women can improves ourselves, become better women, become better humans and living the life of our dreams.